CAMAS & SAGE

A Story of Bison Life on the Prairie

DOROTHY HINSHAW PATENT

ILLUSTRATED BY CHRISTINA WALD

The mission of American Prairie Reserve is to create and manage a prairie-based wildlife reserve that, when combined with public lands already devoted to wildlife, will protect a unique natural habitat, provide lasting economic benefits, and improve public access to and enjoyment of the prairie landscape.

The author thanks the many people who helped with this project along the way, including Damien Austin, Pat Azlin, Dennis Jorgensen, Dennis Lingohr, and Wes Olson.

Thanks to the John and Kelly Hartman Foundation for helping make this book possible.

Library of Congress Cataloging-in-Publication Data

Patent, Dorothy Hinshaw, author.
 Camas and sage : a story of bison life on the prairie / Dorothy Hinshaw Patent ; illustrations by Christina Wald.
    pages cm
 ISBN 978-0-87842-641-6 (pbk. : alk. paper)
 1. American bison—Juvenile literature. I. Wald, Christina, illustrator. II. Title.
 QL737.U53P36 2015
 599.64'3—dc23
                                    2015030622

PRINTED IN HONG KONG

MP Mountain Press
PUBLISHING COMPANY
P.O. Box 2399 • Missoula, MT 59806 • 406-728-1900
800-234-5308 • info@mtnpress.com
www.mountain-press.com

For William Muñoz, who loves bison

This book chronicles the story of a fictional bison calf born on the American Prairie Reserve. Through her first year of life, and by way of sidebars describing various aspects of prairie life, readers will experience this amazing landscape and learn about the iconic North American bison.

Wild prairies once dominated the Great Plains, which occupied roughly the central third of North America, from southern Canada all the way into northern Mexico. Now, with 98 percent of that wild habitat gone, the American Prairie Reserve is working to restore a portion of these vast grasslands in central Montana, just north of the Missouri River, to a fully functioning ecosystem. Currently the reserve covers about 300,000 acres and is visited by more than 60 mammal species and 250 species of birds. The reserve is home to many species of North America's native wildlife, including bison, pronghorn, grouse, prairie dogs, bald eagles, and mountain lions.

A key element in the reserve's effort is bringing back the American bison, also called "buffalo," a species that is not only a symbol of the Wild West but an animal whose activities affect every other species that lives on the prairie. Countless millions roamed across the Great Plains in the not-to-distant past. Today wild bison number in the thousands. A major goal of the American Prairie Reserve is to allow its steadily growing bison herd to live as naturally as possible on the restored prairie, helping return the region to its natural condition of healthy biodiversity. Most bison today have some cattle genes left over from interbreeding, but the reserve's herd is as genetically pure as modern science can determine.

Thundering Hooves!

It's hard for us to imagine the feelings early white explorers experienced when they first encountered gigantic bison herds on the prairie. They could hear the animals coming from miles away. At first the sound was dull, like distant thunder. As the bison got closer, the rumble transformed into the distinct sound of trampling hooves mingled with the moaning of thousands of animal voices. Then the explorers could see a dark-brown tide of bodies pouring over a rise. A herd could be twenty miles wide and more than fifty miles long and take days to pass by.

"I don't know what to compare them with, except fish in the sea," wrote one early explorer. Altogether, there were thirty to sixty million bison in North America when white explorers arrived in the 1700s. By 1900, only twenty-three wild bison were left in all of North America with another 250 in zoos and on farms.

EARLY ON A CHILLY MAY MORNING, a bison cow named Sage plods along the rough prairie ground away from the herd. She feels something moving inside her. She lowers her front legs, plops down on the ground, and rolls onto her side. Her muscles contract, pushing a baby bison out of her body. The protective, sack-like membrane that holds the calf, named Camas, breaks as she slips from her mother's body. Sage stands up and turns around, lowering her head to lick away the shiny membrane. Then she licks Camas all over, using her tongue to fluff up her calf's cinnamon-colored coat.

The Brightly Colored Calf Coat

Bison calves are born with a beautiful cinnamon-colored coat. There may be different reasons for the color. Some people think it allows calves to blend in with the dry prairie grasses of early spring, making them nearly invisible to predators. Others believe this bright coloration makes it easy for protective cows to see their young when they are mixed in with the herd. By about ten weeks of age brown hairs start to replace the cinnamon ones, so the coats start becoming darker and more like those of the rest of the herd.

Bison and Native Americans

The Plains Indians depended on bison not only for food but also for tools and clothing. A bison was like a "walking department store" because almost every part of the animal had some use. In addition to nourishing meat and fat, hooves and horns became drinking cups. Bones became sleds. Tails became fly swatters. Bladders became water vessels. Hides were turned into clothing, bedding, and tepee-making material.

Before Spanish explorers brought horses to America, Plains Indians hunted bison in several ways. Sometimes they stalked the animals, luring them closer by wearing the skin of a buffalo calf. Large groups of Indians would drive bison into makeshift corrals called pounds or stamp them over cliffs at buffalo jumps.

When European Americans arrived, they almost drove bison into extinction, destroying the major natural resource for the Plains Indians. Today, many tribes are establishing their own bison herds, reviving their relationship to these powerful animals.

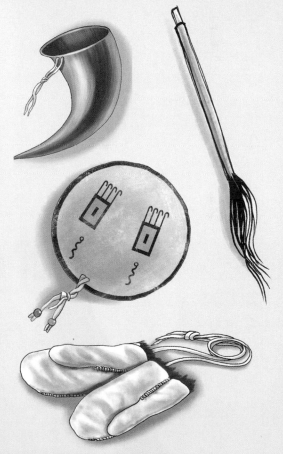

Walking and Running

Like other ungulates, bison have a split hoof formed from two toes. Each toe has a hard, tough coating. Bison also have what are called dewclaws. These extra "toes" help support the animal by spreading out in deep snow or on soft ground, preventing the bison from sinking deeper. The bison's legs may look too small for its body, but they allow this massive animal to turn on a dime. You don't want to get too close to a bison; despite their bulk they can run thirty-five miles an hour! Unlike cattle, bison walk as they graze, so they don't tend to nibble whole patches of grass down to the roots, as cattle do.

Camas struggles to stand. First she tries to get her hind legs to work. Up comes her rear end, but she falls down. Then she tries her front hooves, but down she goes again. Only eight minutes after being born, she struggles to get both her front and hind legs to straighten out beneath her. Soon her legs support her, and there she is, wobbly but standing up on the wide-open prairie that will be her home for the rest of her life. Sage nudges Camas, encouraging her to find her mother's udder. Soon Camas is nursing hungrily on warm, nourishing milk.

"Buffalo" or "Bison"?

The popular name for the American bison is "buffalo," but this animal is not closely related to true buffalo, which live in Africa and Asia. The American bison's scientific name is *Bos bison* or *Bison bison*. Its only close relative is the European bison (*Bos bonasus*), also called the wisent. Scientific names are special names that scientists give to animals. Because each species receives its own unique name, people around the world can be certain they are talking about the same species.

Even though it isn't scientifically correct, the word "buffalo" is used frequently to refer to bison, often in describing things such as buffalo wallows or buffalo jumps.

After just an hour and with a full tummy, Camas scampers along, following Sage as she walks back to join the herd of mothers and calves. Camas sticks close to her mother's side.

Sage doesn't let Camas stray very far. If she senses danger, Sage grunts to warn her daughter to come close. She also makes sure to place her protective body between her calf and any possible threat.

Wolves

Before European Americans settled the prairie, wolves were a particular danger to bison calves. Settlers hunted wolves extensively during the 1800s and early 1900s until they were gone from most of the United States, along with the bison. Wolves were eliminated from Yellowstone National Park, and only twenty-three bison survived there. Yellowstone is now home to as many as five thousand bison. In 1995 wolves were reintroduced into the park, where they have thrived. So far, the Yellowstone wolves have preyed mostly on elk, but some have been relearning how to hunt their larger ancient prey, the bison.

Social Network

The American bison is a social animal, living in groups that vary from a few dozen to up to two hundred animals. The gigantic herds of the past formed mainly in the summer, when hundreds of these smaller bands came together for mating. In the fall, the massive herds would once again break into smaller herds. Mature bulls stay together in loose groups or live by themselves, except during the mating season.

The cows and calves live in organized herds. Each individual has a particular social position. In this story, Sage is the lead cow of her herd. She is an older individual who knows the lay of the land, such as where to find water and where the most protected gullies are for winter survival. She also knows where each member of her herd stands in the herd's hierarchy. Because calves learn from their mothers and inherit some of their genetic traits, calves tend to inherit their mother's status.

Sage and Camas live with other calves and their mothers, away from adult bulls. Sage leads the herd. She knows where the best grazing is, and she makes sure there's always water nearby.

Yearlings and some two-year-olds had been living with the cows, but they went off on their own when the mothers began giving birth. Soon after the new calves are born, some of the younger bison rejoin the herd and stand guard, placing themselves between any threat and the mothers and calves.

Bison Senses

Bison have a powerful sense of smell. They are able to detect the presence of water from at least three miles away. A good nose also helps them detect predators, such as wolves, if the wind is right. Their sense of hearing is also very good.

Bison are prey animals. That means other animals hunt them for food. Like other prey animals, bison have eyes positioned on the sides of their heads. They can see what's happening on both sides of their body and partway to the back and front. In addition, when a herd is grazing, bison face in different directions. This way the herd is likely to detect threats from any direction. Bison are especially good at noticing movement, which alerts them to potential predators.

Camas nibbles the grass now and then, but her mother's milk is what really feeds her. At first she stays close to her mother's side and nurses often. But bit by bit, Camas's curiosity

leads her away from her mother. She scampers over to a nearby calf and sniffs it. The other calf dodges her and heads back to its mother's side, not yet ready for play.

A few weeks after Camas is born, Sage leads the herd up onto a rocky plateau that overlooks the wide prairie. As they graze, the bison face in different directions so they can see danger coming from any side. The calves now spend some of their time chasing one another and butting heads.

When a car full of people approaches, Sage raises her head and stares at the intruders. She's not sure what's going on. The other cows also hear the sound and look up. Sage decides it's best to move on. She grunts loudly to warn Camas to join her. Then, making sure her calf is at her side, she turns and quickly leads the herd away from the humans.

Camping on the Prairie

The American Prairie Reserve features many tepee rings, which are circles of stones the Plains Indians used to stake their tepees down. Many visitors are drawn to the reserve for the opportunity to connect with these historic sites. Tepee rings are often found on high ground.

Camping on a rise in the land made sense. From such a vantage point the Indians could see both prey, such as bison, or enemies, such as a rival tribe, from a long distance. A windswept ridge also keeps down the number of the pesky mosquitoes that plague the prairie in the summer. Wood is scarce on the prairie, so the Indians depended on bison manure, or "patties," for fuel. The patties could most easily be found on the relatively bare slopes, which didn't have as many plants growing on them.

As Camas and the other calves grow, they play more often, running and jumping over sagebrush and shrubs. Their muscles grow stronger as they exercise. They butt heads in play fights and then collapse on the ground to nap.

Sometimes the mothers wander off to find lush grass to eat, leaving their calves with a babysitter to watch over the group. Bit by bit the calves are less dependent on their mothers.

Prairie Plants

The prairie is not just a big field of grass. Dozens of plant species live here, including more than thirty species of grass and over one hundred kinds of flowering plants. Drought tolerant sagebrush is common on the short-grass prairie, such as that of the American Prairie Reserve, and a variety of wildflowers decorates the landscape during the spring and early summer. The prairie is far from treeless. Its trees grow mostly near water and shelter animals such as deer and bison during bad weather.

Bison feed mostly on grass, but other animals prefer different foods. Pronghorn eat more flowering plants and shrubs than grass, whereas elk vary their diet depending on the season. Prairie dogs eat whatever plants grow around their burrows. Doing so clears their view of the prairie, allowing them to see incoming danger.

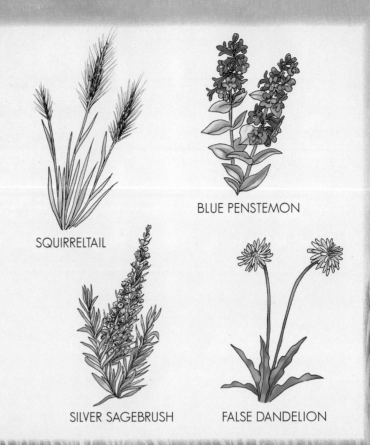

SQUIRRELTAIL

BLUE PENSTEMON

SILVER SAGEBRUSH

FALSE DANDELION

As they graze their way across the land, the bison make grunting sounds that help them stay in touch. One afternoon the sky gets very dark. A sudden flash of light alarms Camas. *What's that?* She wonders. Then a deafening BOOM

shakes the ground. Camas hears Sage's grunt and hurries back to her side, where she feels safe. The herd turns to face into the stormy wind sweeping over the prairie as sheets of rain feed the thirsty grass.

One day Sage leads the herd to a strange place. Camas's curiosity quickly turns to alarm—this place is nothing like the prairie she's used to! There are flat wooden platforms and small wooden buildings. The adult bison scratch their bodies against the platforms to help loosen the remaining patches of their heavy winter coats.

Camas startles at a bright spot of light reflecting from a large metal object near one of the platforms. On the platform a brightly colored hump quivers in the breeze. Camas hangs back from the strange sights. She knows nothing about people, cars, or camping tents. She runs away and huddles close to her mother's side.

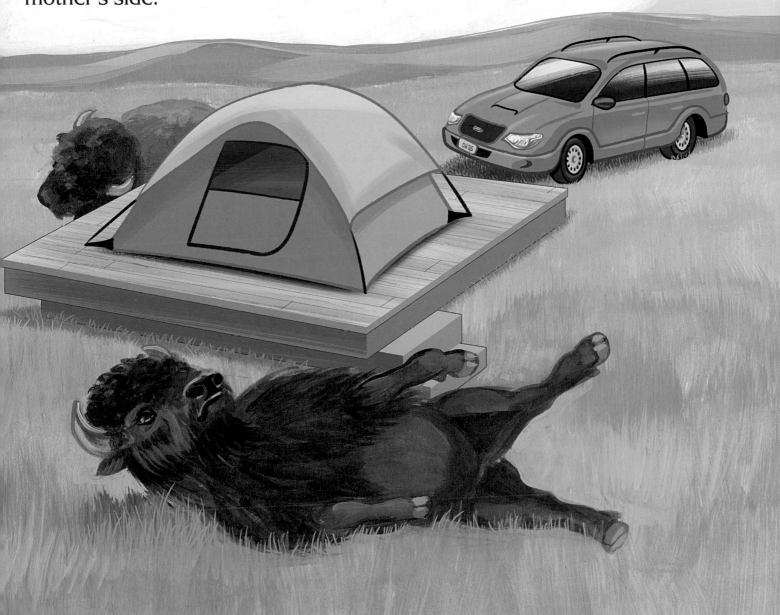

As Sage leads the herd away from the campground, Camas stumbles as her hoof sinks into a hole in the ground. As she rights herself she hears high-pitched sounds and sees small, furry animals scurry away and disappear into other holes. Bit by bit Camas is learning about the prairie and its creatures, such as these prairie dogs.

Prairie Dogs

Like bison, prairie dogs are native to the prairie, and like bison they almost disappeared as farms, ranches, and towns took over their habitat. Prairie dogs are highly social animals who live in colonies that were sometimes huge. In 1901, a biologist estimated that a series of prairie dog towns in Texas covered twenty-five thousand square miles, an area larger than the states of Connecticut, Massachusetts, New Hampshire, and Rhode Island combined! About four hundred million black-tailed prairie dogs lived there.

Prairie dogs eat the tall grass around their burrows. This provides them with food and also clears their view of possible dangers, such as hungry rattlesnakes. Their burrows also provide homes for other animals, including burrowing owls and prairie rattlesnakes.

As spring turns into summer on the prairie, the weather gets hotter. The herd has to cover more ground to find ample grass, but Sage always keeps the group close to water. In the heat of the day she leads the herd to a windy ridgetop, where the breeze helps keep away biting insects.

Bison Coats

Whereas bison calves have a uniform coat of bright cinnamon color, the brown coat of an adult has several different parts that are most obvious during the summer. The hair on the back part of the body is quite short.

A cape of longer fur covers the front part of the body. The upper legs have tufts of hair called chaps, and a definite mane of longer hair hangs down from the neck and forms a beard below the head. A bonnet of thick hair tops the head and hangs down between the eyes. The hair on a bull's forehead is much thicker than that of a cow. The extra hair cushions the blows when males fight. A tuft of hair on the tip of the tail brushes away flies.

In the spring, bison begin to shed their winter coats of long fur. This itchy process takes a long time. They rub their bodies against any object they can find—fence posts, trees, big rocks. Large stones may be polished to a shine by the shedding animals, and trees can lose their lower bark.

Buffalo Wallows

When it's dry, bison roll around on the ground and cover themselves with dust, creating circular patches of bare ground called wallows. The dust helps keep biting insects at bay. It also serves as a rain barrier.

In the past, roughly one hundred million buffalo wallows dotted the prairie, creating variations in the environment that allowed a great variety of plants to grow. They also provided breeding grounds for spadefoot toads. These amphibians spend much of their life buried beneath the prairie. When storms bring two or more inches of rain in a short time, the toads come out and breed. Many choose small ponds that form in buffalo wallows. Their eggs hatch very quickly and the tadpoles grow especially fast so they can mature before the ponds dry up.

Sage finds a bare spot on the ground and lowers her body down. Then she rolls back and forth, stirring up a cloud of dust while Camas watches. Other cows join in, and soon Camas and the other calves are taking turns. Rubbing on the ground relieves their itchy skin.

Camas is growing fast, nursing less often, and spending more time grazing. Her bright cinnamon color fades as chocolate-brown hairs grow in.

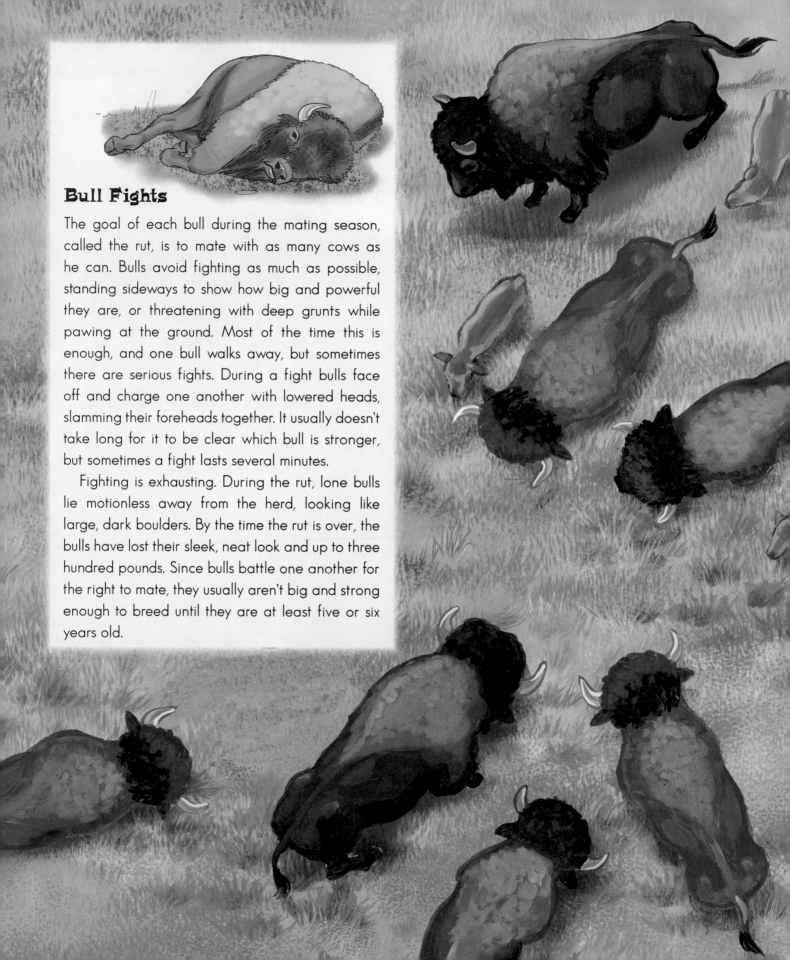

Bull Fights

The goal of each bull during the mating season, called the rut, is to mate with as many cows as he can. Bulls avoid fighting as much as possible, standing sideways to show how big and powerful they are, or threatening with deep grunts while pawing at the ground. Most of the time this is enough, and one bull walks away, but sometimes there are serious fights. During a fight bulls face off and charge one another with lowered heads, slamming their foreheads together. It usually doesn't take long for it to be clear which bull is stronger, but sometimes a fight lasts several minutes.

Fighting is exhausting. During the rut, lone bulls lie motionless away from the herd, looking like large, dark boulders. By the time the rut is over, the bulls have lost their sleek, neat look and up to three hundred pounds. Since bulls battle one another for the right to mate, they usually aren't big and strong enough to breed until they are at least five or six years old.

As the summer goes on, bulls join up with Sage's herd. They are restless. It's time for the rut. The bulls challenge each other by pawing at the ground and bellowing low and loudly—*Hrrrmmmmph!* They fight with one another, banging their heads together and stirring up big clouds of dust. Camas keeps her distance from these violent battles.

One of the bulls approaches Sage, sniffing at her and grunting in a deep voice. Sage leaves the crowded herd and wanders off with the bull. Camas follows her mother but stays out of the bull's way. He sometimes scares Camas by lunging at her when she approaches her mother. But she is still able to nurse and doesn't go hungry.

Tending

A bull can smell when a cow is ready to mate. Once he has chosen her, he leads her away from the rest of the herd. Usually her calf follows. This tending behavior may last for a couple of days until the cow is completely ready to mate.

The bull devotes most of his energy to keeping other bulls away from the cow. Mating itself takes only a few seconds. After it's over, the cow returns to the herd, and the bull turns his attention to finding another mate.

Pregnancy

A pregnant cow has two calves to support—one inside her and one beside her. Pregnant cows begin to completely wean their calves from milk in early fall. By November, most calves depend entirely or almost entirely on grasses for nourishment.

Bison cows usually breed when they are two years old and give birth to their first calf when they are three. Like human moms, babies stay inside bison cows for nine months. This period of time is called gestation. Twins are very rare among bison.

After a few days together, the bull mates with Sage. She and Camas then return to the big herd. Other pairs of cows and bulls come and go, and the bulls keep fighting.

The rut ends by early fall. Now when Camas is hungry for milk, Sage often butts her away and won't let her nurse. Still hungry, Camas eats more grass. She leaves her mother's side to spend more time with the other calves. The young bison soon depend on one another for company because their mothers keep pushing them away.

Chew, Chew, Chew Your Food

Animals such as cattle and bison that feed mostly on grass are called ruminants. Grass is very hard to digest because it is mostly made up of a tough material called cellulose. Ruminants themselves aren't able to digest cellulose, but bacteria and protozoa—invisible organisms that live in their stomachs—do the job for them.

Ruminants have a four-part stomach. In the first part, called the rumen, the food is mixed together and starts breaking down. After a while the animal regurgitates the food, now called the cud. After chewing the cud, which turns the coarse material into a fine mash, the bison swallows it again. This time the cud goes past the rumen and enters the second part of the stomach.

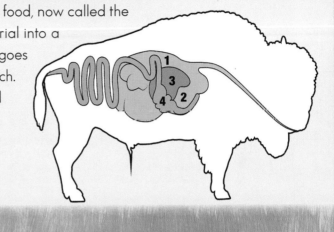

More breakdown takes place in the second part, and water is squeezed out in the third. Now the food is finally ready for complete digestion, which takes place in the stomach's fourth part. After that the food goes through the intestine and is digested even further.

By early fall, all the bulls have left the herd. Sage is once again the leader of her band of cows, calves, and younger bison. Camas and the other calves are now the same color as the adults and blend in completely with the rest of the herd. The bison are growing their longer, warmer winter coats now that the days grow shorter and the nights get colder. Only rarely does Camas try to nurse. She knows Sage is likely to push her away.

Bachelor Bands and Loners

After the rut ends, the bulls wander off. Some loner bulls stay separate from any group. Others form small, loosely organized bachelor bands. Such a band usually consists of bulls of similar age.

Young bulls resemble cows, but during their third summer their coat grows in to look like that of an adult bull. At this age young bulls leave the cow herd and form bachelor bands.

Winter comes fast on the prairie. The wind blasts in from the north, and Sage leads her herd into the protection of a forested ravine as a blizzard hits. For hours cold winds swirl around the bison as they stand facing into the storm. Camas has never felt this kind of cold before, but her thick coat keeps her warm.

The Prairie Winter

Eastern Montana can get really cold in the winter, with lows that reach minus forty degrees Fahrenheit or even lower. Humans have a hard time tolerating these temperatures, but wildlife survives relatively unfazed. Over countless years, wildlife has evolved to take severe cold in stride. Some animals, such as pronghorn and many bird species, migrate south for the winter.

Bison are not the only animals that stick around for the prairie's harsh winter. Elk, deer, and some birds, such as grouse and eagles, remain living above ground. Others, such as prairie dogs, can retreat into their burrows, where the temperature stays above freezing all winter.

Finally the
storm ends. The
sun comes out
but the air is bitterly
cold. Sage breaks trail
through the deep snow,
and the band spreads out
onto the brilliantly white
prairie. Sage lowers her head into
a drift and uses her powerful neck and
hump muscles to shove aside the snow. Camas
does the same, finally moving enough snow to
uncover the grass beneath. She feeds hungrily.

Winter Survival

Bison are superbly adapted to life on the harsh prairie, where the wind can whip through snow-drifts for days. As winter approaches, bison grow a longer, thicker coat that protects them from the frigid days to come. The hair on the back part of a bison's body becomes almost as long as that on the front.

Many animals have difficulty moving through deep snow, but bison are natural snowplows. Their skinny legs move easily through snowdrifts. Using the strong muscles of its hump and neck, a bison can push several feet of snow out of the way to reach the grass underneath. Other animals benefit from bison; they can walk along the paths the bison clear as they feed.

Springtime on the Prairie

When spring arrives, the prairie comes back to noisy life. Greater sage grouse males gather in large groups to attract females with dancing and strange thumping sounds. Prairie songbirds, such as meadowlarks and chestnut-collared longspurs, return from the south, and the males sing to attract mates and declare their territories. Wildflowers burst into bright blossoms as sagebrush sends out sturdy and fragrant shoots, and green sprouts of bunchgrass work their way through the dried-up leaves of the previous year.

Winter lasts a long time on the prairie. By the time spring finally arrives, Sage and the other pregnant cows no longer let their calves nurse. Camas and the other calves hang out together, strengthening their friendships as their mothers withdraw from them. Soon they are living separately from the pregnant cows.

One chilly morning in May, Sage leaves the herd. Her body is telling her that, yet again, she will give birth. As she did with Camas, she licks her new calf clean after it is born and encourages it to find her udder to fill its belly with warm mother's milk.

Camas is now on her own, keeping company with the other yearlings. After all the calves are born, the yearlings rejoin the herd.

As the daughter of a lead cow, Camas knows how to give direction. As she grows older, the other youngsters will look more and more to her for guidance. And one day she will become a leader, just like her mother.

The Future of American Prairie Reserve

Every year the American Prairie Reserve grows with land purchases that help connect the millions of acres of public land already set aside for wildlife and visitors. Staff and volunteers remove fencing that inhibits the movement of wildlife and restore native plants. The reserve's goal is to return more than three million acres of private and public land to its natural state, creating healthy habitat for the native plants and animals that once thrived in the prairie ecosystem. The result will be a park that visitors can enjoy and explore and that also provides employment for local residents.

Longtime Montana resident and PhD zoologist **Dorothy Patent** has devoted her career to writing nonfiction for children. Much of her writing has focused on the West and its history (for example, *Homesteading*, also from Mountain Press) and wildlife (for example, *When the Wolves Returned: Restoring Nature's Balance in Yellowstone*). She has written earlier nonfiction books about the iconic American bison, including *The Buffalo and the Indians: A Shared Destiny*. Dr. Patent has received many awards for her work, including the Washington Post–Children's Book Guild Nonfiction Award, the Orbis Pictus Honor Book Award, and the Edward O. Wilson Biodiversity Technology Pioneer Award.

Christina Wald has done illustration and design for a wide variety of toys, games, books, and magazines. She graduated from the University of Cincinnati with a degree in industrial (product) design. In addition to illustrating *Henry the Impatient Heron* (Mom's Choice Gold Award), Christina's art has graced other children's books, including *Habitat Spy, Little Red Bat, Black Beauty, Big Cats,* and *Do Dolphins Really Smile?* among many others. She lives in Cincinnati, Ohio, with her husband. Learn more about her work at the website www.christinawald.com.